T0317924

Gabriele Tinti
Last Words

Preface by
Derrick de Kerchkove

Images by
Andres Serrano

Afterword by
Umberto Curi

SKIRA

Design
Marcello Francone

Images & Cover
Andres Serrano
images courtesy of the artist

Translation
David Graham & Natasha Senjanovic

First published in Italy in 2015
by Skira Editore S.p.A.
Palazzo Casati Stampa
via Torino 61
20123 Milano
Italy
www.skira.net

© 2015 Skira editore

Printed and bound in Italy. First edition

ISBN 978-88-572-2987-4

Distributed in North America
by Rizzoli International Publications, Inc.,
300 Park Avenue South, New York,
NY 10010.
Distributed elsewhere in the world
by Thames and Hudson Ltd.,
181a High Holborn, London WC1V 7QX,
United Kingdom

Last Words

Preface
Derrick de Kerckhove

I tend to avoid thoughts about suicide. Too many of my friends have done it. Even today when I hear that someone has committed suicide, I have to repress a shudder, a passing moment of anxiety, but that is all. Still, it is quite a challenge to write a preface to this book. I accepted to do it because I have known personally no less than 30 friends or colleagues or members of their families that took their lives. I felt that in some way I owed them the attention that this tragic book gives to the last reflected moment before taking one's life. It is also a challenge to read through these words. Beyond being moving and gravely interesting, they are an invitation to stare at death in the face, something that few among us like to do. La Rochefoucauld wrote among his famous maxims that "Neither the sun nor death can be looked at directly".

And yet, once you resolve to enter into that dark panorama, you cannot leave it. It exerts the fascination of horror. And to that extent, each statement is obscene, not in a prurient sense but, like a grave accident, it is right there, irresistible and "in your face", something you stare at helplessly, comprehending without understanding.

Each sentence is like a still shot before the end. Each text is a recall of a context crushed into a few words, furiously accelerated by the imminence of the end. Reading each one in its emotional variety becomes a renewed but different experience of the absolute limit.

Furthermore, each statement has a "final" character, bearing a summing up of one's life, one's value, one's judgment on self or other. It is in fact quite moving and intriguing, as you go through all of them, to reflect on the difference between those that put the other or the self forward, or those that try to explain or not why they have taken this decision, or still those who through poetry, realism or irony attempt to distance themselves from the imminent act. All, but one, betray a huge level of pain. This one I want to quote in full because, paradoxically, it is the one that brings hope at the core of an act that is perennially associated with the utmost limits of despair: "To all my friends and loved ones, I ask of you one last favor: don't let my spirit die. Remember me for the laughs and the good times, the thrills we all had together. I hope I made a place in all your hearts and touched each and everyone of you in a special way. I have chosen to die, but I have not chosen to be forgotten. I must find a new world, a world of peace and happiness. I want you all to know I am not afraid to die, only to quit living. I'll miss you."

There is beauty here, beauty in the attitude that one can adopt before committing suicide. And, reviewing all of the last words, I am brought to the conclusion that attitude is what brings and carries the suicidal person to the act itself.

Rome, April 5, 2014

Last Words
Gabriele Tinti

I

How much can a man put up with? How much reality can he accept?

In living I die. I'm spent. Broken. I collapse. One hour after another. Moment by moment. Every negative meeting, every crash, every pressure, every opposition, every change. They are all, numerous, *memento mori*. Living as I do I get ready for my death every day, whatever it may be. It is certain that everyone will have his.

A harrowing, crude, disturbing, agonising event, dying. An experience of consciousness, talked about before it's experienced. At times it is written about, a trace of it is left. At other times it is communicated in words. Others still it is silent. In any case it will be for a last time. Because 'reality' as we know it is no longer accepted. It is no more. Because from that point on there is only *death*. Which is definitive. Extorting everything, it splits, lacerates, ends, resolves. Because the door to go there has opened wide. There where there is no longer consciousness, conscience, awareness. There where before there was everything now there is nothing.

II

The imagination, sentiment, 'dear illusions' (Leopardi) make us blind, make us throb, create, shine, sink day after day, they are our life itself. It is the delirium of hope, of believing and lying, that make us carry on as if we should never end. We all live as if forever. But the real experiences are those at the confine, those aroused by suffering, by illness, the only ones able to show us the

9

immense tragedy, to take us back before the icy abyss of the inevitable. But the truly authentic experiences are those at the limits, provoked by suffering, by sickness, by collapse. These are the only experiences capable of revealing to us the immense tragedy of our living unto death, of bringing us to the face of the frozen abyss of the irrevocable. On reaching the brink of that abyss there are those who 'endure to the end' (Rilke) and others who could not put up with enduring or waiting. *Last Words* talks about the latter. The 'guilty'. Because today, as was the case a thousand years ago and has always been, those who commit suicide are considered 'guilty'. Guilty of having sinned against God, against the king and men, against society. Condemned to no longer having their body in the hereafter, because 'tis not just to have what one casts off'.[1] Guilty of having committed a supreme crime. An act of rebellion. Of being anomalies. Suddenly detaching themselves from the collective flow of life – from the continuous chain of love and affection – they isolate themselves, placing themselves against society, against theology, against science. Transgressing their laws they choose egoism, folding into themselves they erase themselves and, in doing so, shun all control. Severing every relationship they test their own limits, fulfil their own desire for tragedy, their own destiny.

III

In *Last Words* I wander around in the cemetery of those who did not make it all the way. Those who decided how to live this 'last', beyond good and evil, by themselves. Men who ended up thinking of suicide in the most diverse ways for the most diverse reasons. Those because of love, or solitude, as an extreme act of extreme awareness, because of an unsatisfied life, or following deep depression, because of an excess of lucidity, because of irreversibly losing that state of exhilaration that is life, because of wanting to finally be someone.

That which emerges is a representation of the *experience of death* that all these people had while communicating it. An ex-

10

perience that is something other than *physical dying*. 'Then came pain and strangulation. This hurt was not death, was the thought that oscillated through his reeling consciousness. Death did not hurt. It was life, the pangs of life, this awful, suffocating feeling'.[2]

Experiences of slavish life, and so without hope, of sorrowful lives, of agonising *Ways of the Cross*; but also of conscious, pathways freed towards the end. Because everyone has his own way of pronouncing the crucial yes to death.

IV

Could their many acts all be unnatural? Certainly they are many acts against. Against the gradual decomposition of the body. Against an enemy, illness, an accident, negative meetings. Against chance. Against the end outside us that comes to meet us. Against God and society. Against their own slow, inexorable decline.

'In the end everything comes down to a fear of death'.[3] And this is why in order to learn to live one should firstly 'learn to die'.[4] Man can be stripped of everything but no one can take away his freedom to kill himself. But 'as yet death is not a festival'.[5] 'Not yet have people learned to inaugurate the finest festivals'.[6] In order to really be free 'for death' and free 'in death' one needs to be a sage capable of saying 'Nay, when there is no longer time for Yea'.[7] For a death in which 'your spirit and your virtue'[8] still shine. Because it is certain that the way of escape lies open before you[9] and death is always at hand, just as it is certain that death, with its gravity and severity, belongs to us 'from the time of our first conception'.[10] It 'rises from the very depth of our self, our essence'.[11] *In proximo mors est*,[12] death is nearby, it is immanent in life, warns Seneca. 'If you do not choose to fight, you may fly'.[13] On the other hand, 'The best thing which eternal law ever ordained was that it allowed to us one entrance into life, but many exits'.[14]

11

[1] Dante, *Divine Comedy, Inferno*, Canto XIII.

[2] London J., *Martin Eden*, CreateSpace Independent Publishing Platform, 2014, p. 297.

[3] Cioran E., *Al culmine della disperazione*, Adelphi, 1998, p. 39.

[4] Nietzsche F., *Thus Spake Zarathustra*, XXI, translated by Thomas Common.

[5] Ibidem, XXI.

[6] Ibidem, XXI.

[7] Ibidem, XXI.

[8] Ibidem, XXI.

[9] Seneca, *Of Providence*, VI, translated by Aubrey Stewart, '*patet exitus*'.

[10] Feuerbach L., *La morte e l'immortalità*, Carabba Editore, 1916-2009, p. 29.

[11] Ibidem, p. 29.

[12] Seneca, *De providentia* (6,9), ed. Alfonso Traina, BUR, 2013, p. 143.

[13] Seneca, *Of Providence*, VI, translated by Aubrey Stewart, '*si pugnare non vultis, licet fugere*'.

[14] Seneca, *Letter to Lucilius*, On the proper time to slip the cable, Letter 70, translated by Richard Mott Gummere, '*Nihil melius aeterna lex fecit quam quod unum introitum nobis ad vitam dedit, exitus multos*'.

Last Words

I

I am not easily beaten, but this time I can see no way out of the black hole.

II

I'm so cold, please do something. I can't stand this empty feeling that I'm having. My head is horrible. Stop the pounding it hurts so much. I have no control over anything in my life. I'm breaking into pieces. Somebody do something.

III

I'm trying to watch TV but I don't know what I'm watching. It's so lonely here. I want to sleep but it just won't come. I'm so tired of hurting and being alone. I keep thinking about the pills in the cabinet but I'm scared. My head hurts so much from crying but if I take anything for it I'm scared I won't stop and I would want to stop.

IV

I don't have any choice in the matter. To make everything better I have to die. I can't make it right by living. I'm so scared I want out but oh I don't know.

V

I don't know how to say this to you but I might as well now as I have nothing to lose.

I've already lost everything. If you're reading this I might have already left or about to leave. I am broken inside. You may not have known this but you affected me deeply to a point where I lost myself in loving you. Yet you tortured me everyday. These days I see no light I wake up not wanting to wake up. There was a time I saw my life with you, a future with you. But you shattered my dreams. I feel dead inside.

VI

I can't eat or sleep or think or function. I am running away from everything. The career is not even worth it anymore. When I first met you I was driven, ambitious and disciplined. Then I fell for you, a love I thought would bring out the best in me. I don't know why destiny brought us together. After all the pain, the rape, the abuse, the torture I have seen previously I didn't deserve this. I didn't see any love or commitment from you. I just became increasingly scared that you would hurt me.

VII

I can no longer put up with being treated as less than nothing, with losing all my friends because of these rumours.

VIII

You tore my soul. I have no reason to breathe any-
more. All I wanted was love. I did everything for you.
I was working for us. But you were never my partner.
My future is destroyed my happiness snatched away
from me.

IX

He's really done it this time. Why didn't I listen to all your warnings and advice? Silly me! So, what now, I keep asking myself?!'

X

I dreamt of our future. I dreamt of our success. I leave this place with nothing but broken dreams and empty promises. All I want now is to go to sleep and never wake up again. I am nothing. I had everything. I felt so alone even while with you. You made me feel alone and vulnerable. I am so much more than this.

I'm not sure why I'm writing this. I went online to look up information on suicide: statistics, methods and all that stuff. I was raised in a family where I went to church every Sunday and was taught the importance of faith and God in our lives. It doesn't matter. It doesn't help me. I got hurt... bad... when I was a child. I was hurt in a way that no person, no little child should be hurt. I think about suicide on a daily basis... sometimes it's all that I can think about. I've been hospitalized for attempts before. I've been put on medications to help the depression... the mental disorders that doctors are so quick to diagnose. I'm sick of it all. Why should I bother trying anymore? I'm not even afraid of dying. I'm not afraid of pain. I just want to leave this world. Please pray for me. I'm tired of trying.

Where will you go, you clever little worm, if you bleed your host dry?

Back in your ride, the night is still young, streetlights push back the black in neat rows.

Off to the right a graveyard appears, lines of stones, bodies molder below.

Turn away quick, bob your head to the seat, as straight through that stop sign you roll loaded truck with lights off slams into you broadside, your flesh smashed as metal explodes.

You may have been free, you loved living your lie, fate had its own scheme crushed like a bug you still die.

Soon, now, you'll join those ranks of dead or your ashes the wind will soon blow.

Family and friends will shed a few tears, pretend it's off to heaven you go.

But the reality is you were just bones and meat, and with your brain died also your soul.

XIII

Send the dying to wait for their death in the comfort of retirement homes, quietly/quickly say "it's for the best", it's best for you so their fate you'll not know. Turn a blind eye back to the screen, soak in your reality shows. Stand in front of your mirror and you preen, in a plastic castle you call home.

Land of the free, land of the lie, land of scheme Americanize!

Consume what you don't need, stars you idolize, pursue what you admit is a dream, then it's American die.

Get in your big car, so you can get to work fast, on roads made of dinosaur bones.

Punch in on the clock and sit on your ass, playing stupid ass games on your phone.

Paper on your wall, says you got smarts.

The test that you took told you so, but you would still crawl like the vermin you are, once your precious power grids blown.

Land of the free, land of the lie, land of the scheme, Americanize.

Now that I have you held tight I will tell you a story, speak soft in your ear so you know that it's true.

You're my love at first sight and though you're scared to be near me, my words penetrate your thoughts now in an intimate prelude.

I looked in your eyes, they were so dark, warm and trusting, as though you had not a worry or care.

The more guiless the game the better potential to

fill up those pools with your fear.

Your face framed in dark curls like a portrait, the sun shone through highlights of red.

What color I wonder, and how straight will it turn plastered back with the sweat of your blood.

Your wet lips were a promise of a secret unspoken, nervous laugh as it burst like a pulse of blood from your throat.

There will be no more laughter here.

I feel your body tense up, my hand now on your shoulder, your eyes...

Forget the lady called luck she does not abide near me for her powers don't extend to those who are dead.

[illegible words] would that I could keep you, let you be the master of your own fate... knowing full well what's at stake?

My pretty captive butterfly colorful wings my hand smears...

I somehow repaint them with punishment and tears.

Violent metamorphosis, emerge my dark moth princess, I would come often and worship on the altar of your flesh... You shudder with revulsion and try to shrink far from me.

I'll have you tied down and begging to become my

Stockholm sweetie.

Okay, talk is over, words are placid and weak.

Back it with action or it all comes off cheap.

Watch close while I work now, feel the electric shock of my touch, open your trembling flower, or your petals I'll crush.

XV

I have fucked up my life again to the point of no return this time. I am homeless, jobless, and penniless. I have 2 wonderful daughters who deserve a lot better than what I can give them, and deserve better in life than what I would ever be able to give them (…). I am in a deep depression and know I will not come out of it.

XVI

What is a few short years to live in hell. That is all I get around here. No more I will pay the bills. No more I will drive the car. No more I will wash, iron & mend any clothes. No more I will have to eat the left-over articles that was cooked the day before. This is no way to live. Either is it any way to die. Her grub I can not eat. At night I cannot sleep. I married the wrong nag-nag-nag and I lost my life.

XVII

i love u... i said it i meant it... i'll love u till the moment i die

devil bin this is the way how i love, perhaps ppl will think it was crazy

i've never tried to put down my pride my dignity my ego-ness on my first ex... but u were totally diff, i put down my pride my dignity my every shit

just to beg u.... but i failed... as always im just a failure in a relation.

XVIII

I have a feeling I shall go mad. I cannot go on longer in these terrible times. I shan't recover this time. I hear voices and cannot concentrate on my work. I have fought against it but cannot fight any longer.

XIX

My fabulous children are my only anchor and I deeply, profoundly regret the pain I will cause them. Please, I beg you, don't hate me for letting you down now.

My love for you both will never disappear because I have no doubts that when you need it, you'll feel it still.

XX

Regardless of what anyone says you'll always be my baby sister. Grab life by the hand or you'll miss out as I will. A million miles away but my family are held close to my heart.

XXI

Cherish every sunrise and cherish every minute. Life can be cruel but some people's lives are mapped out. Can't fight the feelings any more sis. Love you for eternity.

XXII

I am alone this time and no longer able to find the way out. I have no more than despair and fatigue within me now.

XXIII

Forgive me if I'm not strong. I cannot take it any longer.

The time has come for me to move on. I don't come to this decision lightly, however, but now that I'm older, I've finally realized that there's a world of difference between living happily ever after and just living ever after. I may seem strong. But I'm not I'm just like anyone else.

XXV

I am not afraid to die! Who betrayed me and who is worthy, I know clearly in my heart! I no longer want to suffer from unfair treatment! I do not wish to see anyone!

XXVI

Hey, guys, if you're reading this right now, it means I decided to kill myself, but I just wanted to let you know that everything's cool. Seriously, don't freak out! I'm feeling really good about this, and you should, too. Okay, take care.

To all my friends and loved ones, I ask of you one last favor: don't let my spirit die. Remember me for the laughs and the good times, the thrills we all had together. I hope I made a place in all your hearts and touched each and every one of you in a special way. I have chosen to die, but I haven't chosen to be forgotten. I must find a new world, a world of peace and happiness. I want you all to know I am not afraid to die, only to quit living. I'll miss you.

XXVIII

I have no family and no friends, very little food, no viable job and very poor future prospects. I have therefore decided that there is no further point in continuing my life. It is my intention to drive to a secluded area, near my home, feed the car exhaust into the car, take some sleeping pills and use the remaining gas in the car to end my life.

XXIX

My heart has been broken by the people I loved, forgive me but I can't go on. I can only go out like this. Goodbye shitty world.

XXX

Dear Mom, I love you with all my heart. I just wasn't meant for this world! I hope I can find a place of peace and happiness, a place I am child enough to live, yet man enough to survive. I love you! I hope you can truly believe me. Maybe on my journey I'll find Jesus. Pray for me mom. Pray I will find happiness. I hurt so bad inside! I want it all to go away. I want a new beginning. I am not afraid to die mom. I'm just so afraid of tomorrow!

XXXI

I love you, but I can't go on without her.

XXXII

Dear World, I am leaving you because I am bored. I feel I have lived long enough. I am leaving you with your worries in this sweet cesspool – good luck.

Death unknown, The morgue, 1992.

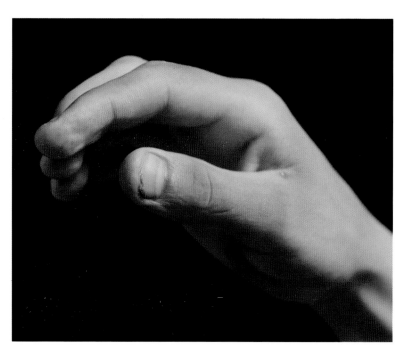

Suicide by Hanging, The morgue, 1992.

II

Rat Poison Suicide, The morgue, 1992.

III

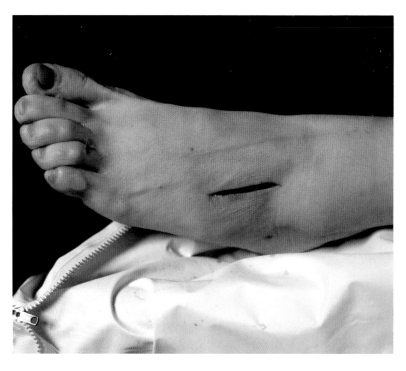

Rat Poison Suicide II, The morgue, 1992.

IV

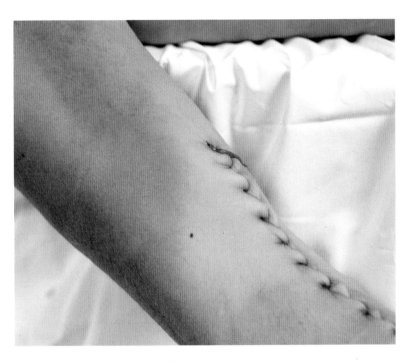

Drug Overdose, The morgue, 1992.

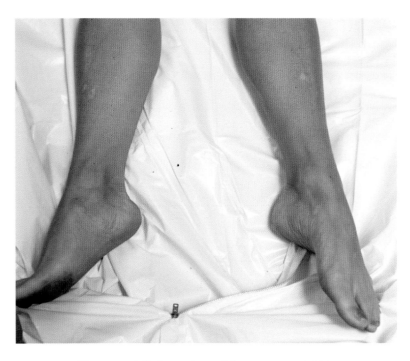

Sleeping Pill Overdose, The morgue, 1992.

Suicide by Pills, The morgue, 1992.

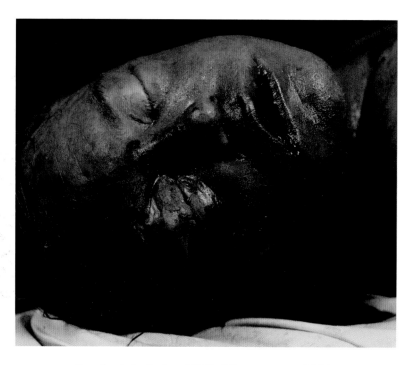

Smoke Inhalation XIII, The morgue, 1992.

VIII

XXXIII

I must end it. There's no hope left. I'll be at peace.

XXXIV

If I can't see my daughter here, I will see her from above...

XXXV

My pain is too strong too strong to handle any longer... Mom here I come.

XXXVI

Take care sis I love you look after them kids until we meet again another time another place.

XXXVII

I'm so sorry everyone forgive me please for what I'm gonna do... This Is It!!!!

XXXVIII

Take two. I hope I get this right.

XXXIX

I'm going to commit suicide. To all of you, even those who shared the slightest friendship with me, I love you.

XL

This life will crash tomorrow!

XLI

I tried. No one listened, I am so sorry. I can't hurt us anymore. Now we are safe. Now we can be happy too. Find it in your heart to forgive me. It's my job to protect him. I know God will welcome our son with open arms. Be happy for him.

XLII

Iv got a plan no one will like it but its gonna happen tonight.

XLIII

I'm going to kill myself and it will be your fault.

I can't go on anymore. I just hung myself.

XLV

Jumping off the GW bridge sorry.

XLVI

I've done my time.

XLVII

The survival of the fittest. Adios Unfit.

XLVIII

Thank you all you have all made an impact on my life some of you good some of you not but you all are loved I hope you all have wonderful lives. I know its not my time to go but I cannot take living any longer. So as of tonight I will end my life. Again thank you for being apart of my life. Merry Christmas.......Good-bye.

My kisses burn into your soul,
My touch melts upon your skin,
My eyes reflect my misery
Of the darkness deep within,
I am a waste of time,
So now I shall die.

L

I'm sacrificing myself to save the countless many who would have to die if I were to live. It's a noble cause, I figure. A good reason to die. I like to think you'd agree.

LI

So that's it. That's me. Leaving the world to be a better place.

LII

Why wait?

LIII

Count down for 45 mins...What should I do in these 45 mins?

You are getting greedy. Act your old age. Relax,
this won't hurt.

LV

I'm happy, Dad. I love you. Goodnight.

LVI

It's my last day.

LVII

Born in San Francisco, became a shooting star over everywhere, and ended his life in Brooklyn... And couldn't have asked for more.

By the time you read this letter, my suicide will be completed. If you have any questions, ask B*** D***. I cared about her so much. My body is at the bottom of the Rt. 82 bridge in the Brecksville/Macedonia area.

LIX

It will be a spectacular event.

Someone call 911. Three dead bodies at 3229 Lima Road Fort Wayne Indiana. I've killed Ryann, Erin, and myself. People were warned not to f——— play me and ruin me. They didn't listen. Sorry about your luck.

LXI

If there's a God then He's calling me back home. This barrel never felt so good next to my dome. It's cold & I'd rather die than live alone.

It's... all... bad... y'all. [puts finger around trigger] ... I love you Mom... I love you Dad... I love you Katherine... God... please forgive me... I'm sorry.

LXII

I hope that my eyes, doused, spark a little love in your heart...
I will be the guardian angel of those who love.

LXIII

She's left me, I'm distraught, I'm shooting myself.

LXIV

I'm arriving in the hereafter.

LXV

Took all my pills be dead soon bye bye everyone.

LXVI

I'm going to put myself to sleep now for a bit longer than usual.

LXVII

Forgive me.

LXVIII

It's time.

LXIX

The End.

Afterword
Umberto Curi

Jack London was right. When you feel pain coming, to the point of suffocation, there is no doubt: it isn't death, it's life. Death does not hurt. Life – with its "pangs" and "awful feelings" – hurts.

These *Last Words* are, simply put, one long, terrible, moving pang. They speak of pain and solitude. They often invoke forgiveness. They reveal the weariness of someone who can go on no longer and chooses to surrender. They are a last attempt at communication by those who are driven to this gesture of no return after having ascertained an inability to communicate. At times they offer a rough explanation of a choice that to most seems inexplicable. They are a plea made with the certainty that it will receive no response, especially because the potential response will no longer find the person who was meant to wait for it.

Aristotle described man as a *zoon logon echon*, a "being imparted with *logos*," to differentiate him from other animals. *Logos*, the word-thought, is thus the principle behind the very definition of the human condition. The word. It accompanies each significant step of our lives. It allows us to express our emotions and decisions, our feelings and appetites, our plans and contemplations. Yet the word is also a message, which implies an equivalent and demands a reply. But when it is a *last* word, when the way back becomes obstructed, it changes meaning. It resembles a cry, something destined to be swallowed up by silence, that no longer forms a *relationship* of any kind, but which falls back onto itself, to be extinguished once and for all in an unending lament.

Myriad ideas emerge from the writings gathered in this book. There are frequent allusions to the relationship between love and death, almost as if emphasis on the latter inevitably reinforced the former. Recurring proclamations of defeat by those who simply can no longer bear life's torments, and thus prefer to face the – ultimate – torment of death. And requests for forgiveness from those left behind. As if some preliminary consent had been necessary for carrying out that gesture. As if those who are left behind could stake a claim on the lives of those who surrendered and chose the path of silence.

Perhaps, however, what most strikes readers who immerse themselves in these writings is the fact that these strange and singular "words," these messages in a bottle destined to remain unanswered, leave us wordless. Suddenly, we realize that we are fragile and exposed, unable to argue, to counter the heralded decision with a warning, an invitation, or advice than can prevent the announced step from actually being taken. This creates feelings of unease and embarrassment, a vague and equally unmistakable feeling of guilt. As if those words constituted an accusatory act, for an offense that we stubbornly, and just as fruitlessly, attempted to dissociate from ourselves.

The great scholar and psychoanalyst Otto Rank offered an explanation – in many ways disturbing – of the subconscious reasons underlying modern funerary practices. The particularly common Western custom of placing the deceased in a casket, sealing it with care and burying it in the depths of the earth, or locking it in a theft-proof burial niche, only partly corresponds to hygienic needs. If we simply wanted to avoid the consequences of rotting cadavers, we wouldn't have to go to such great lengths. Rather, the truth is that overall these practices are dictated by our need to ward off an event that we unconsciously fear: the deceased's return for vengeance. Cemeteries are locked behind tall gates, notes Rank, not to prevent someone from entering, but to keep them from leaving. For even though we're unaware of it, deep down we feel that every dead person is actually a victim – killed by our indifference, our selfishness, our deafness.

The extraordinary writings collected in this book help us understand just how – beyond even the horizon psychoanalysis depicts – all of us, each in our own way, should feel responsible for the fact that *those words* were *last* words. They should teach us *to listen* to the words meant for us while we're still in time to do so. They should exhort us to (cor)respond to *logos* with *logos*, rather than allowing even a single word to be lost like an indistinct echo.

Table of contents